Event Rental Business

Sit Back and Let Your Tables, Chairs, Tents, and Linens Make Money Time and Time Again

Kingsley Pierpoint

By reading this notice, the reader agrees that under no circumstances is the author responsible for any losses, direct or indirect, that are incurred as a result of the use of information contained within this book, including, but not limited to, errors, omissions, or inaccuracies.

Table of Contents

Introduction

If one thing is for certain it's that events will happen. Sure the pandemic might have changed how events operated for a bit, but I think that it is even further evidence that events aren't going anywhere for as long as humans exist. Given that events will occur year-round, you'll be able to make a good full-time income from this opportunity if you stay on track.

Of course, there's a lot that goes into making a business successful and this is no exception. If starting and operating a business was easy, then everyone would be doing it. Look around though and you'll see that most people are working for someone else.

There's nothing wrong with that of course, but part of the issue is finding an opportunity that inherently holds value. Most people are trying to become influencers and the reality is that no fruit will come from it for most people. This isn't something people can consume for free like in the case of social media.

This is something that people have to have, so it puts you in an advantageous position. So let's build off of that. I want you to learn what type of materials you'll need, how to price your rentals, how to optimize things logistically, and of course how to get your phone ringing with eager customers. There's a lot we need to cover here, so let's not waste anymore time.

Chapter 1: Rentals Are Where It's At

As I've already been talking about in the intro, a rental business is where it's at, but not just any rental business, one that involves cheaper items to begin with, and here's why. Imagine you were renting out an RV, trailer, home, or car. These are expensive items. This means your initial start-up costs are higher.

People also don't care as much about your property as you do. They might damage it. Sure they'll be responsible for fixing any damages, but imagine if your RV gets damaged and now you're not able to rent it out to other customers. With an event rental business, things are much different.

For one thing, you can start small and then expand. You can start off with just tables and chairs. This will help to keep your initial start-up costs low.

From there you can expand to provide things such as tablecloths and tents. Tents will be more expensive, but let's say someone breaks a chair.

It's no sweat because you can easily replace the chair and it won't affect future rentals.

With a tent, it will be more costly to replace or repair and this can hinder future rentals. This isn't the only reason for starting an event rental business.

Nobody Wants to Buy a Bunch of Tables and Chairs for Their Event

It doesn't matter what the event is for, if it involves a lot of people, renting is the smart choice. Let's say someone needs 15 tables and 60 chairs for an event. Does it make sense for that person to go and buy the items?

How will they even transport them from the store? Where will they be stored until the event? Where will they go afterwards? Unless someone owns a box truck or van and has extra storage space, it simply doesn't make sense.

By renting, all of the headache is taken care of for the person. The tables and chairs will show up when they need to and they'll be taken away when the event is over. It's as simple as that!

Continually Make Money from the Same Product

Rentals allow you to make money from the same items over and over again. Imagine if you sold tables and chairs. You make the table then sell it.

You have to get another table and repeat the process time and time again. With rentals, you don't have to continually get new inventory. Instead, your inventory will only change every so often.

Over time some items will be too worn down or they'll get damaged beyond repair. Still, though, you'll be able to get a lot of mileage out of your items and make the same amount of profit from a chair that's been used 50 times previously. Think about that for a second. Where else are you going to be able to do something like that?

Great Margins and the Work is Easy

Sure, it is going to take some time to get your money back from buying the tables and chairs. In most cases, your first 5-10 rentals are going to be spent recouping the costs you incurred to buy the items. After that though, the rest is profit that you'll make time and time again from the same items.

The work you're doing isn't that hard either. You drop off some items and then come back and pick them up. It's not like you're having to work the event, do a bunch of manual labor, or anything else like that. The items you have do all of the work for you, you just have to get them there.

Not Hard to Gain Customers if You Know What You're Doing

If you were trying to sell some new product that's never been seen before or some product that's a luxury, you might have a bit of a challenge in doing so if your marketing and sales ability aren't that good. It's easier to sell something that people have to have. And in the case of items needed to put on an event, that's exactly the scenario you're going to find yourself in.

You don't have to try and convince anyone that they need what you have. These are basic items that people are going to need for their event so it really comes down to not messing things up more so than trying to convince someone to need what you have to offer.

Chapter 2: Start Small and Build Your Way Up

In some businesses, it makes sense to be aggressive from the start and go all out. In others, you pretty much have to go all out in order to have any chance of matching up against your competitors. In this realm though, things are much different. I'm going to share with you why it's better to start off small and gradually work your way up as time goes on.

Why Taking Things Step-by-Step is Critical for Your Success

So why is it then that starting small is better in this case than going all out from the jump? Well, there are a lot of important skills you'll get under your belt that you'll need for when you're bigger. One such thing is being able to properly manage your inventory.

This will start to get more complex as time goes on, but by starting small you'll be able to get a better hang of things in regards to inventory management before it starts to get complicated. Your storage and transportation situation will also be easier to manage as well, and your start-up costs will be significantly lower. Let's say though that you did have the capital to go ahead and get all of the inventory you would want.

Should you approach things in this manner? You could if you wanted to, but there's no need to do so. You can instead buy a small amount of tables and chairs, book some events, and then use the money generated from those events to buy more inventory.

This approach is far better than buying a bunch of stock just for it to sit there because you don't know how to market and sell yourself even though you're dealing with something that's easy to sell. I can understand the eagerness behind wanting to go all out from the jump, but you'll be glad you took things slow to start to give you the chance to learn along the way.

Insurance and LLC

Let's cover some of the groundwork for your business. It doesn't matter that you're starting small, you still need to ensure you have the proper coverage from the start so that way you're set up as you continue to grow. So the first thing that you want to take care of is your business entity.

This is totally up to you, but a good choice to consider is an LLC. LLC stands for limited liability company and it helps to create a barrier between you and your company. This is important because let's say someone tries to sue you, with an LLC, your personal assets such as your home or car will be protected and only business assets will potentially be at stake.

You have to make sure though that no one else is using the same business name that you want to use in your state. You can either run a check for this yourself using your secretary of state's website or it will be included as part of a feature for companies that help to create your company entity for you. This isn't the place you want to start though when it comes to a name.

You want to start by checking for domain name availability first. Website domain names are far easier to snag than an official registered business. So your name could be available to establish with your state, but the domain name could be taken and that's not going to do you any good.

This is why you need to check and make sure the .com domain name is available for the name you want to use first. If it is, go ahead and grab it. Domain names are cheap and typically only cost around $15-25 per year to maintain.

Then you can start the registration process for your LLC. If this is something you've never dived into before, then the process can seem overwhelming to say the least. This is why I recommend using a company that can help you out such as Tailor Brands or Legal Zoom.

These companies and others like them make it very seamless to get your company established. The amount it's going to cost you will vary depending on the state you live in. Some will be more than others so be prepared for this cost before you're ready to file.

The other thing you need to think about before your first rental goes out is insurance. Someone could sit on your chair, it breaks and they get injured. You might not properly stake a tent, it blows away in the wind and damages someone's car.

These things are unlikely to happen and I don't mean to scare you by any means, but you have to be prepared for scenarios like these. Insurance coverage isn't going to break the bank, it will help to give you peace of mind, and some people are going to require proof of insurance in order for them to book with you.

General liability insurance is going to be a good place to start, but I recommend working with an agent to help give other coverage recommendations that may be needed to help with your specific needs.

Follow Things in This Order

When it comes to inventory, I recommend that you follow things in this order. Start off with tables and chairs. Then expand your inventory by buying more tables and chairs so that you can serve more people.

You'll learn soon enough that you'll have to turn people down because all of your inventory is booked and you'll want to remedy this situation as quickly as possible. Once you've expanded your table and chair inventory to a point where you feel like you can adequately keep up with market demand, then move onto your next item. The next item that you should look to add to your inventory is going to be tents.

Tents are useful for a variety of weather conditions. They can help to block the sun and with tent walls, they're also great for blocking the wind and cold. So naturally they can help to turn an event that would be miserable into something manageable. The thing with tents is that they tend to not last as long as something like a table.

Even if a table gets scuffed up, it will be covered by a tablecloth in most cases. With a tent, it's easier for the colors to fade from sun exposure and for other damages to occur due to the size and set up and take down. Also depending on the size, it will be harder to transport. If you're dealing with a larger-sized tent, you're going to have to upgrade to a trailer or box truck at this point.

This is why you want to wait and maximize on tables and chairs first. However, in spite of these downsides, being able to offer a tent will give you plenty of pluses. For one thing, some people might not book with you if you don't have tents.

Sure they'll be able to get tables and chairs from you at a lower rate than the competition (more thoughts on this will be expanded upon later), but people still won't be willing to go through two different companies in some cases.

Additionally, you'll be able to rent a tent for a similar price point to what it would cost to buy. On the surface, this doesn't make sense.

When you think about the hassle of the set up, the labor costs, and the fact that people don't want to keep a large tent for similar reasons to excess tables and chairs, it soon becomes easy to see why you can make a great profit margin from tents. As time goes on, you'll want to start expanding your tent inventory. It can be easy enough to start off with a 10x10, and then get a 10x20 and 20x20, etc., even getting multiples of certain sizes.

Once you've done that, you can consider moving on to tablecloths if you want to. Naturally, it would seem that tablecloths would be easier to manage than tents, but a lot of rental companies will subcontract tablecloths from another company. Why is this the case?

Well, the condition of tablecloths matters far more than anything else. They're going to be front and center for everyone to see when they're eating. This creates a big problem though because with a lot of people eating, people aren't going to care and the tablecloths are going to get stained easier than any other rental item you offer, and the condition matters more than any other item.

Therefore, they have to be thoroughly inspected and cleaned after each usage and properly stored so they don't get dirty in between uses. If you're unable to get a visible stain out, then the tablecloth is done for and you'll already have to replace it, which can make the mileage per item way less compared to the other things I've mentioned thus far.

This is not to deter you from tablecloths as the margins are good if you're able to manage the upkeep. I just want to make you aware that you can offer them or subcontract them from another company and make a smaller profit off of them. If you subcontract though, it's less about the profit and more about being able to fulfill a client's needs.

Reinvest Everything Back into the Business

I get that it's exciting to start your own venture and have people pay you for what you're offering. You're going to be working hard for this money so it's natural to want to spend a little bit on yourself. However, it's really important to reinvest everything you can back into the business.

This business can grow exponentially quicker by reinvesting your profits. Reinvesting your profits will allow you to expand your inventory at a rapid rate. You'll then be able to invest in a trailer or box truck and extra storage space.

Sure, these things will cost a lot of money and it will take some time to save up for them, but you might as well start with the extra money you're making. This is of course up to you, but if you want to grow your business, I implore you to live off of your 9-5 and not touch the additional income your business is providing you. This will give you the shortest path to be able to eventually quit your job.

And if you do have a job right now and are considering quitting to start your rental company, I think it's best to thoroughly think through that decision. The reality is that most of your rentals are going out on the weekends, which makes for a seamless fit with a 9-5 job. Quitting your job at the start will only put pressure on you to make a profit now.

And as I talked about earlier, it's going to take a few rentals to get to the break-even point. No matter what it's going to take a few months just to recoup your initial expenses and that's the best case scenario.

If a Customer Wants Linens, Sub Rent

As I talked about a bit ago, you don't want to miss out on a job because someone wants linens with their rental. If a potential customer contacts you and inquires about linens, you don't want to say that you don't offer linens and they'll have to look elsewhere. This will likely lead to you missing out on the business entirely.

Get more information from the customer about what color they're going to need and then form a connection with a linen rental company. You'll rent the linens from this company and then charge more than what you're paying to sub rent them to the customer.

This way you'll still be able to keep the rental job and make some profit off of it. Sure it won't be as much compared to you owning the linens, but this is a great workaround to not owning any linens in the beginning.

Deliver in Your Own Personal Vehicle if Possible

The next way for you to save money with this venture is to use the vehicle you already have. This is doable if you own a truck, van, SUV, or other larger-sized vehicle. If you own a compact car, this will be more challenging to pull off for larger orders.

Even with that being the reality, it doesn't matter because you can make multiple trips to complete the delivery. If you currently don't own a vehicle or a vehicle suitable for a particular job, then ask around in your network and see if someone has a larger-sized car that they'd be willing to let you borrow. If you're unable to do this and you have to rent a van, this will greatly eat into the amount of profit that you're making per job.

While it wouldn't be ideal, it would probably be better for you to go ahead and bite the bullet on something that you can work with now and in the future. For instance, if you bought a used truck, you could use it to transport your loads when they're small. Then as you expand, you can buy a trailer and still continue to use the truck to help complete your drop-offs.

Yes, this will be an additional big expense upfront, but at least the payments are going towards you owning the vehicle instead of just eating up your profits for nothing. What you don't want to do is buy something like a van. Yes, this will be helpful upfront but it will lose value as you start to grow. You'll have to resell it so you can buy a box truck or truck and trailer.

Eventually, Get Your Own Storage Space/Warehouse

As time goes on, the next thing you'll want to upgrade is your storage space. When you're starting out, it's best to save money on storage if at all possible. You may not be able to do this depending on your current living situation.

If you have a home with a garage or shed then these are great options. If not, then consider if you can afford to give up some extra space inside your home to get by. Eventually, the next move would be to get an offsite storage unit that will allow you to get more supplies.

The thing is that you don't have to worry about getting a climate-controlled unit or anything like that based on the items you're going to be storing. Eventually, though, you will outgrow that space. You're going to need to get a warehouse just to store all of your various supplies. By this point, your business is going to be a decent-sized operation.

Your operating costs are going to be higher and you're going to be needing to charge a higher price point at this stage. The main thing you'll want to look for when signing a lease for a warehouse space is going to be flexibility. You want to ensure that you don't get trapped in a long lease if you're ready to expand well before the lease is up.

This can definitely happen and even the opposite can happen where you have more space than you need. So it's best to stay nimble and be able to move easier in exchange for paying more per month. You may come to realize there are certain things you don't like about the warehouse space you're in.

Sometimes you won't be able to determine these things until you're working out of the place. So look for a flexible lease that allows you to get to a month-to-month scenario as quickly as possible. In most cases, you have to commit for a minimum of 3-6 months and then you can go month-to-month.

Some places are only going to want to offer multi-year leases. So it can take a while to find the right sized space at the right price for you. This is why you want to start the journey early when it comes to finding the right spot.

It doesn't hurt to look because you're not committing to anything. You'll have some options in your back pocket so that you can strike when you are ready to expand.

Hire Your First Employee

This is where the fun truly begins. You're going to have so much inventory but only so much time to do things. At this point, you'll be missing out on orders if you don't bring in extra help.

The first role you should hire for should just be there to help you with fulfillment. So they can help pull orders to get them ready, go with you to help with drop-offs if need be, etc. What will likely be the case is that you're not going to jump from zero employees to a full-time employee.

Instead, it needs to be a softer transition where you hire someone part-time. This will help to give you a bit more flexibility in terms of the number of hours they get per week, and their hours can expand along with the business. It can be intimidating to try and hire someone because what if you make the wrong choice?

While that can happen, you have to think about things from a different perspective. What if you don't make a hire and your business continues to miss out on potential revenue because of it?

Chapter 3: Rental Pricing

Determining how to properly price your rentals is something that will make or break your success. Most people don't have a clue how to price their rentals and it hurts their business. You have to find a happy balance with the stage your business is currently at.

For example, if you charge too much, nobody is going to be renting from you. Charge too little and you waste your time and resent your business. What it boils down to is you have to take advantage of the strengths of your business for the stage it's in.

When you're small, your overhead costs are lower, so play to that. When you're bigger your overhead costs are much higher sure, but you have more inventory and can fulfill more orders faster, so play to that.

This fluidity is what will help you thrive when others are struggling. There is some nuance to being able to pull this off so let's go more in depth with it.

Should You Price Similarly, Above, or Below Your Competition?

So you're just starting out, you have your first set of inventory and you're ready to go. In terms of what the market in your area is offering for renting the same items, which route should you go? In the same realm?

Below what everyone else is offering? Or go above what others are charging? The thing is you could get a variety of different answers depending on who you ask.

Here's the path you should take though. You should start off by going as low as you reasonably can. When you're starting off, you have to think about what it is that sets you apart?

You don't have the biggest variety of options when it comes to your inventory. You can't fulfill faster than bigger companies, so what can you do? Well if you come in at a cheaper price point, now you're able to be competitive

People will still turn to you even if you're new and without a good reputation simply because of your pricing. Profit wise, you're still going to be in good shape because your overhead costs are lower. This lower price point is what will help you get your foot in the door and establish yourself.

Your bigger competitors won't be able to offer the same rate as you and that's fine. Their advantage is the variety and amount of inventory they have. All of your inventory will be eaten up after 2 to 3 people book with you and you'll have to start turning people down.

They'll be able to fulfill all of those extra orders. Some will disagree with this and say it's just a race to the bottom when you undercut your competition. I don't see it like that. What you're doing is temporary.

You're playing to the strengths of your small operation. If you were bigger and still doing this, then that would not only hurt your business but the competition as well. There's no need for that as you'll need to increase your pricing as you expand just to keep up with the additional expenses that you're going to incur.

Scope Out Your Competition

So what should you charge? I'm going to give you some price ranges in the next section, but bear in mind that every place is going to be different. If you live in a remote area, rentals are going to be cheaper compared to someone who lives in a big city.

This is why the best place to start when it comes to pricing is to go ahead and look at what your competition is charging. Doing this is easy, simply go to their websites and see if you can find their pricing.

Some people will list it and others won't. If you can't find pricing information on their website, call or email them and pretend like you're an interested customer so that you can gain insight into what they're charging. Once you've gathered enough data, you can now get a general idea for what you need to charge in order to be competitive in the market.

What Are Some General Starting Points?

So if you'd like to get an idea of what you'll need to be charging, a good range per chair rental would be in the realm of $2-$2.50 for fancier chairs, such as white resin. Your larger competitors are going to be charging in the realm of $3-$3.50 per chair, so you'll be a good amount below that.

From the customers' angle, they'll be able to save a good chunk of money by going with you, and you'll just make a good amount of profit. For regular folding chairs, a good starting price point is $1.50-$2. And as far as tables are concerned, charging $10-$12 is a good range for a 6-foot fold-out table.

Get a Deposit

One mistake you'll want to avoid making is not collecting a deposit. Maybe you already know this from previous jobs or business ventures, or possibly even from dating, but people are flaky. They'll contact you and be all excited about the rental only to cancel on you.

This is a major problem because your inventory is tied up when it could be going out to someone else. So essentially you're going to miss out on business entirely if someone cancels on you. This is where the deposit comes into play.

You need to collect a nonrefundable deposit in order for someone to book with you without exception. The inventory is not officially tied up until the deposit is paid. If someone tries to give you an excuse of putting down a deposit once they get paid on Friday or whatever else, that's great, but if someone wants to pay a deposit for the same date before Friday then the rental goes to them.

Again people are going to say stuff like they'll pay the deposit on Friday and then you'll never hear from them again. So if you keep the inventory on hold, then all you're doing is holding back for someone who hasn't even committed to you yet.

How Big of a Deposit Should You Require?

This is your business at the end of the day, so you can do what you want. I will however offer you some guidelines. I would recommend that you charge at least a 20% deposit, but preferably you would go with 50%.

The thing about a deposit is that it's not going to be a dealbreaker for most people. They'll know they need the items so if they make the decision to book, they'll expect a deposit and they won't balk at 20% vs 50% in most cases.

If you feel more comfortable going with something in the 20% realm, then, by all means, do it. Just know that if they cancel, you now have your inventory tied up for only 20% of the full rental price when you could have at least gotten half.

Where Should You Buy Your Inventory From?

When it comes to buying your initial inventory, you have a couple of options. You can buy new or you can buy used. If you go the new route, it will obviously be more expensive, but your items will be in great condition and will last longer than if you buy used.

However, there is a trade-off to buying new. The trade-off is that if you buy used you'll either save money or you'll be able to buy more inventory with the same amount of money you're using to buy new. This is why I believe buying used is a good route to go so long as you're patient.

The reason why I say this is because you never know what you're going to get condition-wise when it comes to buying used. Sure, the price may be great but that doesn't matter if you're buying items that you'll only be able to rent out a time or two. Most of the pictures in people's listings aren't going to do justice in most cases.

A lot of dents, stains, and the like can easily be covered up or not seen in a low-quality photo. You have to do your due diligence and check out the items in person. Unfold the chairs and sit on them.

Thoroughly inspect the tables, and most importantly don't be afraid to walk away if the deal isn't right. The chances of every chair and every table being a good fit are slim. You can offer to leave bad tables and chairs out of the deal and see if you can get a lower price.

Most people though will just want to get rid of their entire stock, so be prepared for that. When inspecting the items you have to decide how bad the damage is. Is it something that you can touch up or repair yourself?

Or is the item a goner? What you don't want to do is buy something that isn't usable because now you're stuck with the items. With a bit of patience though you can find a good deal with most of the items being in good condition.

It's worth it to have to wait a week or two to find a good deal because if you pay more your first rentals are just going to be covering more of the start-up costs anyways.

Delivery and Pickup or Just One?

Another thing to consider is offering an option for the customer to choose between delivery or pickup. Having the customer do a pick-up themselves can save you a lot of hassle, especially if your transportation situation isn't ideal for this business right now.

So you'll definitely want to offer that as an option for willing customers. Most people though will prefer that you deliver the items to them. This is totally reasonable, but you can tack on a delivery fee in these cases if you want to, such as $30 or $40.

Chapter 4: Maintaining the Quality of Your Items

One of the biggest keys to success with a rental business is taking care of your equipment. The longer you're able to make your items last, the more profit you'll ultimately end up making from each item. There are some steps you can take to help stretch out the lifespan of your items, so let's cover those things now.

Take Pictures Before and After Each Rental

Yes, doing this is going to be a little bit tedious, but it will allow you to know the condition of your items before and after each event. This is important so that way there's no misunderstanding between you and the client. You'll be able to show them up-to-date photos of what their items will look like, and you'll be able to tell if they were brought back to you in a condition much worse than what you sent it in.

What I recommend is marking each of your items with a number in a spot where it won't be seen, such as underneath the table or chair. If you have 100 chairs, for instance, you can label each one 1 through 100. Then you can take photos of each chair before they get rented so that you have a reference point.

Now if a dispute does arise, you'll be able to show the customer what the condition looked like before they rented it. If you only do sporadically, such as after every 5th rental, then you won't be able to prove which client is responsible for the damage. This gives you evidence to show that a chair was not damaged before the client rented it, for example.

You could of course skip this step if you don't mind replacing damaged or broken items yourself, but I still think it's good to be able to show your customer an updated look of what their items will look like.

Inspect the Returns as Soon as Possible

When you're at the event picking up the items, this is not the time when you want to be inspecting your returns. Instead, this is something you'll want to do on your own time, but you'll want to do it as soon as possible. Yes, it can be a pain to have to go back through everything, but if a discrepancy does pop up, you'll want to be able to address it right away.

There might also be some other marks and scratches on some of the pieces that you'll want to try and touch up anyways, so it's a good idea to do this sooner rather than later. It can be easy to forget about inspecting the items, they then go back out to the next customer, and the next thing you know, you get a complaint because something was off and you were never able to catch it. Upon doing an inspection it will be normal to come across some scratches or marks on your tables and chairs.

So what should you do when you come across these things? Well, the first thing you can do is try and use a melamine foam sponge and see if you're able to remove any of the marks with that. These work surprisingly well at removing misccllaneous marks that can accumulate over time on your items.

It's also a good idea to spray your items with a cleaner that can help to prevent scratches as well as cleaning off your tables with disinfectant spray. This isn't something you need to apply after every single use, but it is something handy to use after every 3 or 4 uses or so.

These are the main things that I would try and do before the items go out so that the customer is satisfied with the way the product looks. You'll also help to separate yourself from your competitors who are lazy and won't inspect their own items.

Getting an Agreement in Place

So let's say that you do get something like a chair back and it's completely broken, or a table that isn't able to be used again. What do you do in these scenarios? Well, it's best to get an agreement in place with the customer to best ensure that your business stays protected.

You could of course just eat the cost, but that isn't fair to you and it will hurt your business in the long run, similarly to not collecting a deposit. When it comes to drafting up an agreement, this is something that's best to hire an attorney for.

They'll be able to draft up a proper agreement that you'll know will have all of the correct verbiage and language usage. But what are some of the things you'll want to be sure that are included in your agreement? Here are a few things you may not have thought about:

What Will Constitute the Customer Being Responsible for Replacing an Item?

If you get some basic scratches or marks on your items, this should be expected and the customer shouldn't be responsible for having to replace your items or pay for damages in these instances. What the customer should be responsible for is if an item isn't repairable and isn't able to be used again. Yes, this can create controversy, but it's your business and you have to protect your assets at all costs.

If not, then you're going to be the one replacing a broken table, for example, and that's money coming directly out of your profits. Luckily though, you're not dealing with items that are super expensive, so your customers should be understanding especially if they know that something happened that caused one of your items to completely break. My cousin is a DJ and one time a guest spilled their drink all over her equipment and had to pay to get it cleaned.

All of her notches were completely sticky and wouldn't move smoothly like they did before. Now that is thousands of dollars worth of equipment here and since she works every weekend, that created a sticky situation, to say the least.

You likely won't deal with an extreme scenario like that. Even if you have a few chairs broken that you'll need for a quick turnaround for your next rental, you can always replace the items yourself until you get reimbursed.

Sick or Unable to Complete the Delivery

Something else you need to think about in your agreement is if you're unable to complete the delivery. What if you get sick, have a family emergency, car troubles, or something else that you can't predict pop up that causes you to be unable to complete the delivery? You need to help shield yourself in these rare instances just in case.

So you'll want to make sure that your agreement has a section in it that covers the unfortunate event that you're unable to complete the delivery. This might include having someone else complete the delivery if available or having to cancel the order.

The Details of the the Request

There are many details that you'll want to have nailed down about the day to ensure that there's no he said she said going on. For example, you might agree to a certain location over the phone. Then you get there and no one is there because the wrong address was given to you. Now you end up arriving late and a dispute starts with the customer.

This type of situation can be avoided if you get in writing the certain details from the customer. In this case, if it was in writing where the items would be delivered to, then it can clearly be shown why you went to the original address that you did and what caused you to be late. Here are some of the details about the rental that you'll want to be sure you get in writing:

-Customer Pick Up or You Dropping Off

-Location of Drop Off
-Drop Off Date
-Drop Off Time
-Customer Name and Contact information, such as phone and email address

Taking care of these things will help to give you something to fall back on so that way there's no misunderstanding between you and the client. Anything that's said over the phone can create a possibility of someone forgetting to mention a detail and that's when chaos can occur. Here are some other things you'll want to think about as part of your agreement:

Deposit

As I said before, you want to collect a deposit for your rental because you don't want someone eating up a prime weekend spot just to cancel on you last minute for nothing. You'll want to be sure to put this in as part of your agreement in case the customer asks for a refund. You'll be able to point to the fact that they signed and agreed to no refunds being given so this is an important thing to include as part of your agreement.

Reschedule Policy

Sometimes dates will change and the customer may need to change the date they originally planned on needing your items. You need to a have policy in place for what you will and will not accept. For instance, your policy may be that the customer has to give at least a 48-hour notice and can only be moved if there is still availability.

If you're unable to move due to already being booked up on a certain day, then you won't be able to fulfill the customer's request. You can also charge an additional fee for this as well. For example, you could charge an additional 25% to move the rental to another date.

The reason you would do this is because most likely you won't be able to rent your items out in that short of a time frame, so you're still missing out on profit you would have otherwise had. By charging a rescheduling fee, you help to recoup some of the money you would have made that day. The last option you have is to not allow any sort of rescheduling for a different day under any circumstance.

The customer would just have to eat their deposit and then rebook with you for a different day. This can be a bit harsh on the customer service side of things, which is why I prefer an approach that's a bit more lenient, but still very beneficial towards your business.

And the cool thing about this is that the customer won't sign if they don't agree with your way of doing things, so you might as well keep policies in place to help prevent a customer from taking advantage of you on purpose or incidentally.

Refund Policy

This is the part of the contract where you'll want to explicitly state that refunds won't be offered under any circumstances once payment is made. Yes, unforeseen things happen, but you're a business and you have to protect that as best you can. Going back to my cousin dj, one time she was djing a wedding and the couple broke up before the wedding started!

She just got all of her equipment set up, and then a fight broke out between the couple. They ended up calling off their wedding! My cousin left without rendering the service, but by that point, it didn't matter.

She already showed up, unloaded all of her equipment, and was ready to go. She also had received all of the money for the gig and the couple understood that they weren't going to be getting their money back. As part of your refund policy, you need to lay down the rules very clearly by stating that in order for a date to be booked, a deposit of 50% (or whatever your number is going to be) must be put down.

Then the remainder must be paid at least 48 hours in advance from the pickup date. It's important to spell out when the other 50% is going to be due because you don't want to be stressing out at the last second trying to get your money.

Customers will try to push things to the limit with this if they can, so it's important to have the details very clearly laid out, so that way the customer knows how to act.

Chapter 5: How to Increase Your Rental Bookings

When people start a business, they typically don't think about being in the sales and marketing business. However, with any business you start, you have to be able to do those two things in order to be successful. You have to be able to properly market your business for people to know that you exist in the first place.

Then you have to be able to guide them into booking a rental with you. Those things can be hard to accomplish if you don't have any prior experience with them. Fortunately for you, this chapter is going to help ensure that even if you don't have experience with these things that it won't be an issue for you.

Two Things Matter Above All Else

When it comes to this business, there are two marketing methods that are far and above the rest. Make no mistake about it, there's virtually an endless amount of ways that you could try and spread the word about your business. Doing marketing activities though doesn't mean that it's going to drive bookings at the end of the day.

You have to narrow down your focus to what will give you the biggest bang for your buck. Remember, you're a busy person and you probably don't have 40 hours a week to dedicate to marketing your business. That's totally okay.

What you need to do is have things set up in place that bring leads to you consistently without you having to put in a continual amount of effort.

So what are the two best ways to gain exposure for your brand new business? It's going to be running advertisements on social media and search engine optimization, or SEO for short. You'll notice that I said running ads on social media and not necessarily posting on social media. Yes, you should still create business profiles and post on them on a regular basis. You should also post on any personal profiles that you have and let your friends know about the business you're starting.

That's an easy way to get the ball rolling. Your new business social media accounts are going to start with zero followers. Think about how long it's going to take to start getting some leads from all of the effort that you're putting in.

Think about how low your engagement will be and how few people will actually be seeing what you post. Yes, it will happen, but it's going to take some time. You need something that will help to get you bookings today.

The same thing applies to SEO. Initially, you're not going to be ranking very high, but it's a long-term strategy that you need to be investing in from day 1, because once you do start to rank high, leads will easily and effortlessly flow to you without paying anything or doing anything extra. I don't know about you, but that sounds like a worthy time investment.

Still though, to get a spark going day 1, it likely won't do much unless there isn't a lot of competition in your area. So ads are where it's at. You can immediately pay and be put in front of people who can become potential customers. The major downside to ads is that, yes, they will cost money, but you can still be effective even with a small budget.

If you were running radio ads, then this would not be the case. Your expenses would be higher, that's for sure. Luckily with social media ads, you can choose whatever kind of budget works for you, so let's go ahead and talk more about running some ads.

Running Social Media Ads

Not only do I like running ads on social media specifically because of how you can easily make it fit your budget, but so many people are on social media. It's hard to find someone who has never used social media before. This means that people who are in need of chairs, tables, tents, and other such rentals will be on social media.

The other thing I like about social media ads is that you can get specific with who you target. This way your ad isn't being randomly shown to people who aren't going to care.

You can give yourself the best chance possible to drive leads from your actions. In order to be effective with this though you have to know who it is that you want to target.

Who is the Ideal Type of Person to See Your Ad?

If you don't know who you want to ideally see your ad, then it will fall flat on its face. The first step to running a successful ad campaign is to stop and think about the person whom you want your ad to appear in front of. So in this case, what are some reasons people would need to rent some tables and chairs?

A wedding would be an obvious one. A party such as a birthday party, corporate party, or retirement party would be some other good options. Family reunions and city events are another potential reason people would need to rent out some tables and chairs. So once you've thought of some different types of people who would be interested, it's time to move to the next step.

Segment each different group of people

Now what you're going to want to do is run a separate ad for each group that you're targeting. Why would we do this? It's because it will give us the opportunity to split test each group of people and see which one results in the highest return on investment. This doesn't mean you're only going to target one interest per ad because that will likely be too narrow.

But rather, you would take the type of person, such as someone who's engaged, and group a few interests together that fit the bill for that type of person. So if you were targeting 4 different groups of people, instead of being broad and trying to target all 4 groups at once, you'd instead run 4 separate ads. You'd also split up your budget accordingly.

Instead of spending your entire $20 daily budget on one group, you'd split it up by spending $5 on each of the four different groups. Within each group you can target multiple aspects, such as gender, age, things that they are interested in, job title, and of course, location. Location is a critical piece you don't want to forget.

The last thing you want is for someone to be interested but because you didn't set any radius for a location, they live in another state and you wasted your money. You can get very narrow or broad with each ad that you run as you can see. Don't let the unlimited number of possibilities intimidate you though.

Running ads is about testing and tweaking. You're not going to run the perfect ad from the start, but things will get better as you're able to test and get more data. Also, keep in mind that the main thing you want from an ad is a high click-through rate.

Click-through rate is the percentage of people who saw your ad and clicked on your link to be taken to your website. This is absolutely huge. This means someone was on social media, you interrupted them and got them to leave the website they were on to go somewhere else. That's huge and it doesn't happen that often.

There are different average click-through rates depending on the industry you're in. A 5% click-through rate would be amazing to achieve, but you can still be profitable with even a 3% click-through rate.

So think about that, 95% of people who are shown your ad will continue to scroll and not move to your website. The 3-5% that do, however, will make all of the difference. So what are some different interests and job titles you could consider targeting to get you started? Well here are a few ideas:

-Wedding venues
-Caterers
-Event planners
-Administrative assistant
-Secretary
-Receptionist
-Flower Shops
-Jewelers
-Dj
-Event manager
-Production manager
-Hospitality
-Bakeries

So this is a bunch of different things, and if you lumped them together, you likely wouldn't get very far. Instead, you can take some of these ideas and lump them together to form a better-fitting profile.

So let's take one category such as a bride and groom-to-be. What are some different interests we could lump together to start testing an ad? The following would be some good ideas:

-Wedding venues
-DJs
-Bakeries
-Flower Shops
-Jewelers
-Caterers

Now that we have our categories, we can set our location and gender to target both males and females, and be ready to go. Let's look at another example using a food caterer.

Sure, most caterers will likely have some equipment, but if they get a big gig they likely will need to rent to make up for what they don't have. Also, someone who's just starting out may prefer to rent the necessary supplies to be able to serve people. So here are some categories to consider:

-Caterers
-Bar-b-q
-Food
-Restaurant

Continuing on, let's say we want to help target event planners. One obvious category for this one would be the job itself. You could also target other similar jobs along with this, such as secretaries or receptionists who may also be tasked with helping to plan for an event.

Aside from this, you could also target things such as organization and other things that relate to organization, such as calendars, ink pens, sticky notes, etc.

Having categories simply isn't enough though, you need to set your budget for each category and then test things out to see how it goes. You likely won't have a profitable ad right from the jump, but what you can do is tweak things to help improve your ad as time goes on. So how long should you let an ad go on for before you decide to tweak things?

Well if you immediately jump the gun after 24 or 48 hours, then that is too soon. The algorithm is still learning its way and will better optimize as time goes on. What you don't want is to ditch an ad that could have been profitable but you gave up on it too soon.

It's better to know for sure that something isn't working rather than leave too soon. This is why I recommend waiting at least two weeks before you decide to make any changes to your ad. Now based on the data you see, you can make some changes.

For example, let's say that you have a low impression rate, such as 6%. This means that the ad itself isn't engaging, such as the picture or text that you're using, or that your categories are off because your ad is being shown to the wrong type of person. The best way to figure out the sticking point is to run variations of the same ad. So you'll make another ad where you change just the picture you're using.

Then another ad where you try some different copy for your ad. The same type of premise applies to your categories. Run ads where you eliminate or add one interest at a time.

There's a very good reason why you only want to change one variable at a time. If you change multiple things at once and your ad does better, then how do you know what caused the improvement? By testing one variable per ad, you'll know if your new version does better or worse.

If you test a new picture and it does better than your old picture, stick with the new picture. If you try some different text variation that does better, now you can combine that with your new picture for an even more effective ad. You'll continue to test variations until your ad is fully optimized.

Yes, I know that this sounds like a pain and that's because it is. It's not necessarily fun to continually tweak and optimize things. It would be better if you could throw an ad out there and make money from it. That simply isn't how things work.

The best ads are the ones that have been split-tested hundreds of different ways. You don't know what a fully optimized version of your ad looks like and that's okay because neither does anybody else with ads they're running! That's what testing is for.

And the good news is that you don't have to do 100 different split tests to at least be profitable. You can achieve profitability relatively quickly and then continue to improve your profits by further optimizing your ad. Being successful with ads really comes down to being patient.

If you expect to immediately make money, you will set yourself up for failure. You'll start to pull the plug early on your ads without thoroughly testing them. You'll get frustrated and wonder why things aren't working.

Instead, if you approach things with a mindset of patience, then you won't get upset when you "lose money", instead, you'll know that every dollar you spend is worth it because it gives you data that you can use to help make better-informed decisions to further optimize your ad.

Search Engine Optimization

The second best way to generate leads for your business is to rank high in search results. This can take a while to rank at the top of your area depending on how much competition you're up against. But there are some steps you can take to ensure that you're properly preparing yourself for success.

The first step is to create a Google My Business account. This will allow your business to appear in the search results when someone searches the phrase "table and chair rental," for example. Think about what happens when you type in something, such as "dentist near me."

A bunch of different dentist offices will appear in the search results, and this is what will happen once you create a profile. Initially, though, you won't have any sort of track record so you'll be at the bottom of the results, but as time goes on and you start to accumulate more reviews, your ranking will start to increase. So how do you go about getting reviews?

Well anytime someone rents from you, you need to be willing to follow up with them multiple times if necessary, using multiple avenues to get the review. Most people aren't going to think to leave a review, so you have to ask. Text them and send out an email.

If they don't leave a review, wait 2-3 days and kindly remind them again. Doing this is really important as it will help to establish trust with other people who are interested in renting from you, as well as helping out your ranking. You also want to ensure that your website is optimized to help answer customer questions and help make it easy to find the info they're looking for and book with you.

Another key aspect to ranking higher is load time. If you have a slow load time, your bounce rate will be high and this will hurt your rankings. If however people come to your website and don't continue to search for other related things, then this shows that the search request was satisfied and it will help out your rankings if this is a continued pattern.

Lastly, one other thing that can help with your ranking is backlinks. This is when another website links your website somewhere on their website. Obviously though, getting backlinks from just any website doesn't necessarily make a difference.

The more established a website is, the better the quality of the backlink is. It would be better to get one high-quality backlink than 100 weak ones. Backlinks though can be difficult to achieve.

The best strategy is to reach out to other websites and see if they'd be willing to feature you on their website. Most of the time they won't be interested unless you are willing to pay for the feature. It might not be a bad idea if the website has a relevant audience.

You don't want to pay for something like this purely for the backlink. You'd want to generate some leads from it as well.

Chapter 6: How to Easily Manage the Booking Process

One of the most important factors to having a successful business and keeping your sanity is to ensure that you're properly organized. You want to make things easier for everyone involved.

You want to make it easy for the customer to book with you and you want to make things easy on yourself. In this chapter, I want to share with you some things to think about to help with your booking process.

Manual is Okay to Start but Look to Build in Automation from the Jump

When you're first starting out, you're not going to be contracted left and right for bookings. This is okay because it allows you to get your ducks in a row. You can start off with more of a manual process in the beginning

So you can keep track of your inventory using a speed sheet and manually tracking what inventory is booked up and what is available for different dates. However, soon after you get going, you'll want to start the process of making things more automated.

Imagine if instead of manually tracking things, which can lead to the possibility of human error, that instead you have your website do all of the heavy lifting for you. Someone can come to your website, and see what you have available and what you don't. Then when they book, your website will automatically update the inventory count.

Not only does this make the process more seamless, but it can make your job easier. Instead of people contacting you and asking what you have available and what you don't, it can all be seen on your website. In order to implement something like this I recommend hiring a web development company or freelancer who can help to make this a part of your website. This will cost a good bit of money, which is why I recommend you start saving your profits early on so you can make this happen as soon as possible.

Have Multiple Ways for People to Book

Even though your automated website will be your main form of booking once it's implemented, you'll still want to give people as many options as possible to book with you. For example, let's say someone sees one of your posts on social media and sends you a DM. It would make sense to just book them right then and there since you're dealing with a hot lead.

If you send them to your website, they might not get the info they need, get frustrated, and leave. So in cases like this, you're still going to manually book rentals, but you're doing so when it makes sense. It's not just your websites and DMs though.

Be sure to take phone calls and emails, as well as additional methods, for people to book. The more options you give to people, the more likely it is they'll book with you. This way you'll ensure that your business has a method that works for everyone.

The younger generation might not like talking on the phone and would prefer to book directly on your website or via DM. An older generation might not feel comfortable navigating technology, so a phone call would be better for them to get their questions answered.

Have High-Quality Pictures of Your Items

Do you want to know how you can easily separate yourself from your competitors? Ensure that you have high-quality photos on your website. So if you have 3 different kinds of tables and 3 different kinds of chairs you're currently renting out, make sure you have high-quality photos of each different type so that people know exactly what they're getting.

High quality also builds trust because it makes your items stand out compared to someone else whose pictures make you doubt an item's functionality. If you really want to go above and beyond, hire a professional photographer to ensure you get good photos. If you're taking the photos yourself, the best advice I can give you is to ensure that you have proper lighting.

You don't want any shadows to be cast over your items. So you can either take your picture outside on a sunny day or you can buy some cheap studio lights to help create good lighting in your own home.

Have an Updated List of Items if You Aren't Automated Yet

Even when you're doing things manually, it's still a good idea to have an up-to-date list on your website so that way people know what you have before they contact you. This can help to cut down on people reaching out, just for you to not have something. Instead, when people reach out, they'll already know what you have available.

The trick is that you have to constantly keep the list updated. It can be easy to forget to update your website after someone books, but forgetting will ultimately lead to a frustrating customer experience. So as long as you stay on top of things, this can be a big time saver when you're in the beginning phase.

Conclusion

A rental business is one of the easiest and best businesses that you could start. All you have to do is drop off some items and get paid. Who doesn't love the idea of that?

Your success with this business comes down to your ability to stay organized. It would be easier to do that in the beginning, but as time goes on, it will be more of a challenge to manage more inventory and deal with more customers.

As long as you have a solid foundation building upon that will be easy. There will be challenges ahead but I know that you can do it as long as you believe in yourself!